The Quotation Bank

Blood Brothers

Willy Russell

Copyright © 2020 Esse Publishing Limited

First published in 2018 by:
The Quotation Bank®
Esse Publishing Limited

10 9 8 7 6 5 4 3 2

All rights reserved. No part of this publication may be reproduced, sold, stored in a retrieval system or transmitted in any form, or by any means (electronic, photocopying, mechanical or otherwise) without the prior written permission of both the copyright owners and the publisher.

A CIP catalogue record for this book is available from the British Library.
ISBN 978-1-9999816-1-7

All enquiries to: contact@thequotationbank.co.uk

Printed and bound by Target Print Limited, Broad Lane, Cottenham, Cambridge CB24 8SW.

www.thequotationbank.co.uk

Introduction

What examiners are looking for	4
How The Quotation Bank can help you in your exams	5
How to use The Quotation Bank	6

Quotations

Act One	7
Act Two	19

Revision and Essay Planning

Major Themes and Characters	32
How to revise effectively	33
Sample essay, potential essay questions and revision activities	34
Glossary	41

Welcome to The Quotation Bank, the comprehensive guide to all the key quotations you need to succeed in your exams.

Whilst you may have read the play, watched a production, understood the plot and have a strong grasp of context, the vast majority of marks awarded in your GCSE are for the ability to write a focused essay, full of quotations, and most importantly, quotations that you then analyse.

I think we all agree it is **analysis** that is the tricky part – and that is why we are here to help!

The Quotation Bank takes 25 of the most important quotations from the text, interprets them, analyses them, highlights literary techniques Russell has used, puts them in context, and suggests which quotations you might use in which essays.

At the end of **The Quotation Bank** we have put together a sample answer, essay plans and great revision exercises to help you prepare for your exam. We have also included a detailed glossary to make sure you completely understand what certain literary terms actually mean!

English Literature 9-1: What are examiners looking for?

All GCSE Exam Boards mark your exams using the same Assessment Objectives (AOs) – around 80% of your mark across the English Literature GCSE will be awarded for A01 and A02.

A01	Read, understand and respond to texts. Students should be able to: <ul><li>Maintain a critical style and develop an ***informed personal response***</li><li>Use textual references, ***including quotations***, to support and illustrate ***interpretations***.</li></ul>
A02	Analyse the ***Language, Form and Structure*** used by a writer to ***create meanings and effects***, using ***relevant subject terminology*** where appropriate.

Basically, **AO1** is the ability to answer the question set, showing a good knowledge of the text, and using quotations to back up ideas and interpretations.

AO2 is the ability to analyse these quotations, as well as the literary techniques the writer uses, and to show you understand the effect of these on the audience.

We will also highlight elements of **AO3** – the context in which the play is set.

How The Quotation Bank can help you in your exams.

The Quotation Bank is designed to make sure that every point you make in an essay clearly fulfils the Assessment Objectives an examiner will be using when marking your work.

Every quotation comes with the following detailed material:

Interpretation: The interpretation of each quotation allows you to fulfil **AO1**, responding to the text and giving an informed personal response.

Techniques: Using subject-specific terminology correctly (in this case, the literary devices used by Russell) is a key part of **AO2**.

Analysis: We have provided as much analysis (**AO2**) as possible. It is a great idea to analyse the quotation in detail – you need to do more than just say what it means, but also what effect the language, form and structure has on the audience.

Use in essays on…Your answer needs to be focused to fulfil **AO1**. This section helps you choose relevant quotations and link them together for a stronger essay.

How to use The Quotation Bank.

Many students spend time learning quotations by heart.

This is an excellent idea, but they often forget what they are meant to do with those quotations once they get into the exam!

By using **The Quotation Bank**, not only will you have a huge number of quotations to use in your essays, you will also have ideas on what to say about them, how to analyse them, how to link them together, and what questions to use them for.

For GCSE essay questions, these quotations can form the basis of your answer, making sure every point comes directly from the text **(AO1)** and allowing you to analyse language, form and structure **(AO2)**. We also highlight where you can easily and effectively include context **(AO3)**.

For GCSE questions that give you an extract to analyse, the quotations in **The Quotation Bank** are excellent not only for revising the skills of analysis **(AO2)**, but also for showing wider understanding of the text **(AO1)**.

Act One:
   MRS LYONS: "It's a pretty house isn't it? It's a pity it's so big. I'm finding it rather large at present."

Interpretation: The wealth inequality between Mrs Lyons and Mrs Johnstone (and in society in general) is clear. Mrs Lyons doesn't grasp the true value of what she has.

Techniques: Adjectives; Adverbs; Nouns.

Analysis:
- Mrs Johnstone describes the house as "lovely", suggesting an appreciation of the house's qualities as a family home – Mrs Lyons uses the adjective "pretty", depicting a more superficial appreciation of the house and its appearance.
- The adverb "so big" emphasises the scale of the Lyons' wealth, yet Mrs Lyons calls it "a pity" – the audience see Mrs Lyons as ungrateful, as well as insensitive to the plight of Mrs Johnstone and the working class.
- "Finding it rather large" continues the idea of ingratitude, but also implies that Mrs Lyons is painfully lonely, setting up her later quest for a child.

Use in essays on... Class; Wealth; Nature vs Nurture.

Act One:
> **NARRATOR:** "There's shoes upon the table an' a joker in the pack, the salt's been spilled and a looking glass cracked, there's one lone magpie overhead."

Interpretation: The audience are introduced to Mrs Johnstone's superstitious beliefs, all of which seem to revolve around avoiding bad luck rather than embracing good luck.

Techniques: Language; Sibilance.

Analysis:
- The narrator's list of superstitions are all negative in tone – "cracked" and "spilled" involve breakages and accidents, "lone magpie" stresses isolation, and the image of it lurking "overhead" creates a lingering sense of foreboding.
- The "joker" has associations with mischief and trouble, and the fact it is hidden "in the pack" suggests fate could deal this mischief at any time – we are powerless to stop it.
- The sibilance of "salt's been spilled" accentuates the speed with which things can go wrong – one small mistake and things spill out of control.

Use in essays on… Fate and Superstition.

Act One:

> **MRS JOHNSTONE:** "They say I'm incapable of controllin' the kids I've already got. They say I should put some of them into care. But I won't."

Interpretation: There is pressure on Mrs Johnstone to control her "kids" in a socially acceptable manner; if she can't, society will act swiftly and coldly to remove them.

Techniques: Repetition; Sentence Structure; Language.

Analysis:
- The repetition of the pronoun "they" implies a nameless, faceless bureaucracy controlling the lives of the working class, made particularly threatening when it even controls innocent "kids".
- The vague "some of them" and callous "put" dehumanises the children – whilst Mrs Johnstone loves them all as her "kids", the "Welfare" see families and working class human relationships as simply a logistical problem.
- The single clause sentence "But I won't" has a strong and defiant tone in the face of social pressures from those above her.

Use in essays on… Class; Family and Relationships; Wealth.

Act One:
> **MRS LYONS:** "I must have my baby. We made an agreement, a bargain. You swore on the Bible."

Interpretation: Mrs Lyons' sense of entitlement is evident in her claiming of the baby, as well as her manipulation of Mrs Johnstone with the idea of religious condemnation.

Techniques: Nouns; Tone.

Analysis:
- Although not as explicit as the physicality and guns of later scenes, the tone of "I must have" and the ironic "my baby" are equally as violent and aggressive as the physical intimidation shown by Sammy.
- The nouns "agreement" and "bargain" stress the clinical, business-like approach Mrs Lyons takes to secure herself a family – it contrasts with the much more chaotic, but more natural, scenes in the Johnstone household.
- "Swore" and "Bible" are ways for Mrs Lyons to justify her behaviour, as if she has a religious validation for demanding the child.

Use in essays on… Fate and Superstition; Violence; Family and Relationships.

Act One:
MRS LYONS: "These brothers shall grow up, unaware of the other's existence. They shall be raised apart and never, ever told what was once the truth."

Interpretation: Mrs Lyons preys on Mrs Johnstone's superstitious nature to create fear and get her own way, but also coldly articulates the true nature of their deal.

Techniques: Abstract Nouns; Juxtaposition; Language; Irony.

Analysis:
- "Brothers", with associations of unbreakable family bonds, is juxtaposed with "raised apart", highlighting the immorality of the women's decision – it is of course painfully ironic that the exact opposite of Mrs Lyons' statement occurs.
- "Truth" should suggest an unalterable fact, yet "what was once" implies "truth" can be manipulated to fit the needs of those with power in society.
- The depth of the deceit is shown in the use of "never, ever". The imperative "shall" alongside "unaware" stresses the extent of their manipulation over other human lives.

Use in essays on… Family and Relationships; Truth; Nature vs Nurture.

Act One:
NARRATOR: "Y' know he's gonna find y', Y' know he's right behind y', He's starin' through your windows, He's creepin' down the hall."

Interpretation: These lines re-occur throughout the play with ever increasing intensity; each time the devil gets closer, more aggressive, and a step nearer to claiming his debt.

Techniques: Prepositions; Verbs; Language.

Analysis:
- The narrator reaffirms the unavoidable nature of the tragedy in the play. "Y' know" and "gonna" confirm that the devil will eventually get them; however, it is not simply Mrs Johnstone and Lyons who suffer, but everyone around them.
- The prepositions "behind", "through" and "down" create a sense of a hunter (the devil) stalking its prey, slowly and methodically closing in.
- "Starin'" and "creepin'" increase the atmosphere of tension and inevitability amongst the audience; by Act Two the devil has "moved in down the street", "wants to speak to you" and is "leanin' on your door".

Use in essays on… Fate and Superstition.

Act One:
EDWARD (*awed*): "Pissed off. You say smashing things don't you? Do you know any more words like that?"

Interpretation: Differences between the brothers are clear in the language they use. Later on, Mickey envies Edward's education, but Edward envies Mickey's freedom.

Techniques: Register; Juxtaposition; Questioning.

Analysis:
- The vulgar "Pissed off" juxtaposes the more refined "smashing", with the different registers stressing the class differences between Mickey and Edward.
- Whilst the working class may be envious of the middle class and their "big houses", the stage direction "awed" suggests Edward is impressed with the independence Mickey has to say what he likes and act how he pleases.
- "Do you know" emphasises that although Edward may be formally educated in a world containing "the dictionary" and "the meaning of words", Mickey has a knowledge of the real world that Edward will never share.

Use in essays on… Class; Education; Truth; Wealth; Nature vs Nurture.

Act One:
   CHORUS: "You can get up off the ground again, it doesn't matter, the whole thing's just a game."

Interpretation: The innocence of youth conflicts with the symbol of the gun throughout the play – a gun is both a toy in a playful game, and a deadly murder weapon.

Techniques: Language; Foreshadowing.

Analysis:
- "Off the ground" highlights the childish rules of a make-believe game, but also foreshadows the end of the play when Mickey and Edward can no longer get "off the ground" as they are blown away by exploding gunfire.
- The joyful associations of "just a game" suggest their games are not significant, but they evolve into a life of violent crime and, in Sammy's case, murder.
- Whether the audience believe fate and superstition are responsible for the outcome of the play, essentially "it doesn't matter", as life is nothing more than a vague "thing" over which we have no control.

Use in essays on… Fate and Superstition; Violence.

Act One:
POLICEMAN: *"Well, there'll be no more bloody warnings from now on. Either you keep them in order, Missis, or it'll be the courts for you, or worse, won't it?"*

Interpretation: The Law is not a fair system that treats everyone impartially, but rather it discriminates against the working class, seeing them as the root of society's problems.

Techniques: Language; Sentence Structure; Tone.

Analysis:
- The policeman, a representative of the justice system, sees it as acceptable to use rough, intimidating language ("bloody warnings") and patronising, degrading terms ("Missis").
- Mrs Johnstone and her family are not even identified as individuals – she is a nameless "Missis", and her children are simply referred to as "them".
- A constant threat hangs over the Johnstone family. The sentence structure creates an ominous tone, stressing the something "worse" than "the courts" awaiting the Johnstone family – something inflicted by society, not fate.

Use in essays on… Class; Family and Relationships; Justice; Wealth; Nature vs Nurture.

Act One:

> **POLICEMAN:** "An' er, as I say, it was more of a prank, really, Mr Lyons. I'd just dock his pocket money if I was you. (*Laughs*)"

Interpretation: The difference between classes is accentuated by the interactions with the policeman; the same "crime" is treated very differently between Edward and Mickey.

Techniques: Sentence Structure; Language; Tone.

Analysis:
- The multi-clause sentence creates a tone of subservience towards Mr Lyons, and the submissive tone of "An' er, as I say" suggests the policeman is socially inferior. His role is to protect the middle class and punish the working class.
- What was violent, adult law-breaking for Mickey has morphed into a childish, amusing game for Edward, highlighting the class discrimination in the legal system. Also, Mickey's mother is a "Missis", Edward's father is "Mr Lyons".
- The intimidating threat of "courts, or worse" has become a gentle docking of "pocket money", and Mickey's "serious crime" has become Edward's "prank".

Use in essays on… Class; Justice; Wealth; Nature vs Nurture.

Act One:
> **MRS JOHNSTONE:** "Shush, shush. Listen, listen Eddie, here's you wantin' to stay here, an' here's me, I've been trying to get out for years. We're a right pair, aren't we, you an' me?"

Interpretation: Just as Edward is about to leave, the audience are shown a scene of true tenderness between mother and son, accentuating the agony we feel at their separation.

Techniques: Register; Repetition; Pronouns.

Analysis:
- The informal use of "Eddie" emphasises a more natural connection, whereas Mrs Lyons' register when talking to her son seems formal and detached.
- The repetition of "shush, shush" is tender and loving – not only does Mrs Johnstone provide physical comfort for Edward, but the repetition of "listen, listen" highlights the maternal guidance she also provides.
- The use of "pair", "we" and "you an' me" stresses the familial bond between Mrs Johnstone and Edward – they are far closer than he is with Mrs Lyons.

Use in essays on… Family and Relationships; Truth; Nature vs Nurture.

Act One:

MRS JOHNSTONE: *"Ey, we'll be all right out here son, away from the muck an' the dirt an' the bloody trouble. Eh, I could dance. Come here."*

Interpretation: As Act One concludes, fate seems to tease the audience – whilst Mrs Johnstone seems overjoyed, we know she is moving back, once again, towards Edward.

Techniques: Irony; Tri-colon (or List of three); Language.

Analysis:
- It is the persistent nature of life's problems that wears Mrs Johnstone down – the tri-colon suggests these problems are unpleasant and demeaning ("muck" and "dirt") as well as harmful ("bloody trouble").
- The irony of moving to the country to avoid "muck" and "dirt" is clear – Mrs Johnstone does not mind the literal "dirt" of the countryside, but rather it is the metaphorical "muck" and "dirt" that plagues her.
- The Johnstone family don't ask for much, simply to be "all right", and her optimistic outlook on life is accentuated by the dynamic "I could dance".

Use in essays on… Family and Relationships; Wealth; Fate and Superstition.

Act Two:
MRS LYONS: "We have had a very good time this holiday though, haven't we?"

Interpretation: Whilst Edward appears to enjoy a privileged lifestyle with parents who love and care for him, there seems to be a desperation in Mrs Lyons' need to please him.

Techniques: Alliteration; Adverbs; Language.

Analysis:
- Compared to the Johnstone family, Mrs Lyons and Edward seem awkward together. "Have had" creates a tone of falsehood, with Mrs Lyons determined to believe they have had a "good time", as well as anxious for Edward to agree.
- The adverb "very" accentuates this point – it is not enough for Edward to enjoy himself, but rather it has to be a "very" good time to reinforce what a perfect family they supposedly are.
- Whilst "haven't we" could be seen as a simple question that is seeking agreement from her son, it also has a tone of desperation – Edward is forced to agree to calm his increasingly unstable mother.

Use in essays on… Family and Relationships; Truth.

Act Two:
CONDUCTOR: "But you've got to have an endin', if a start's been made. No one gets off without the price bein' paid."

Interpretation: The outcome of the play is made explicit to the audience. There is no way to avoid the inevitable consequences of the decisions made earlier in Act One.

Techniques: Alliteration; Juxtaposition; Language.

Analysis:
- The working class all face the same desperate fate – "gets off" has associations of criminality from which "no one" is innocent, as highlighted earlier in the different treatment the policeman exhibited to Mickey and Edward.
- The lack of control Mrs Johnstone has is clear – her life is a pre-written story with a "start" and an "endin", and there is no way she can influence the outcome fate has in store for her.
- Alliteration emphasises the harsh reality of the world – "price" and "paid" both stress that society is cold and money-driven.

Use in essays on… Fate and Superstition; Class; Wealth.

Act Two:
EDWARD: "I know but I still can't tell you. It's not important. I'm going up to my room. It's just a secret, everybody has secrets, don't you have secrets?"

Interpretation: Edward's refusal to tell his mother his secret, or to hand the locket over to his teacher, emphasises the strength of the bond between him and Mrs Johnstone.

Techniques: Dramatic Irony; Repetition; Language.

Analysis:
- The childhood innocence of "going up to my room", "it's not important" and "just a secret" are contrasted with the importance, significance and guilt of Mrs Lyons' secret.
- Edward's question "don't you have secrets" creates a painful dramatic irony – the audience know Mrs Lyons' secret and are fearful its inevitable consequences will end in disaster.
- The repetition of "secrets" reinforces the underlying tension of the play; any potentially positive developments are tainted by the underlying deceit.

Use in essays on… Superstition and Fate; Truth; Family and Relationships.

Act Two:

MICKEY: "I wanna kiss y', an' put me arms around y' an' kiss y' and kiss y' an even fornicate with y' but I don't know how to tell y', because I've got pimples an' me feet are too big an' me bum sticks out an'…"

Interpretation: Mickey's feelings for Linda come tumbling out, but his uneducated, inexperienced nature means he is unable to express himself in the way Edward can.

Techniques: Repetition; Polysyndeton; Juxtaposition.

Analysis:
- Mickey's repetition of "kiss" emphasises his youthful naivety. He does not have the sophisticated vocabulary of Edward, and cannot easily articulate his feelings.
- Mickey's use of polysyndeton mimics the fact that, as he enters adolescence, his life becomes uncontrollable, seemingly slipping from his grasp.
- The juxtaposition of the formal "fornicate" with the immature tone of "pimples" and "bum" emphasises the conflict between childhood and adulthood.

Use in essays on… Class; Education; Nature vs Nurture.

Act Two:
KIDS: *"High upon the hill the mad woman lives, never ever eat the sweets she gives."*

Interpretation: The sophistication, class and elegance Mrs Lyons had in Act One has disappeared. She is now a figure of ridicule and mockery for the local children.

Techniques: Alliteration; Language.

Analysis:
- The alliterative "high upon the hill" stresses Mrs Lyons' increasing isolation – she wanted a baby so she could feel loved and needed, but has ended up even more alone than she was previously.
- This is accentuated by the use of "the mad woman" – the singular "the" further develops the sense that Mrs Lyons is isolated and lonely.
- A great deal of sympathy can be felt for Mrs Lyons – the "sweets she gives" are clearly a desperate plea to entice children and company into her life, but instead have turned her into a caricature, a fairy-tale monster.

Use in essays on… Class; Family and Relationships.

Act Two:
NARRATOR: *"And who'd dare tell the lambs in Spring, what fate the later seasons bring. Who'd tell the girl in the middle of the pair, the price she'll pay for just being there."*

Interpretation: As "the lambs" hurtle through adolescence, experiencing love, life and sex for the first time, the audience are aware their childhood will soon be over.

Techniques: Symbolism; Language; Alliteration.

Analysis:
- The reference to the trio as "lambs" symbolises their innocence and purity, but also alludes to the metaphor of 'lambs to the slaughter' – Mickey and Edward will end up being sacrificed to pay the "debt" their mothers owe.
- "Spring" signifies fresh potential and endless possibilities; however, due to the agreement made by Mrs Lyons and Mrs Johnstone, fate will inevitably "bring" consequences so devastating no one "dare" mention them.
- The plosive alliteration of "price she'll pay" is violent and aggressive – fate will destroy everyone, even a young, vulnerable "girl".

Use in essays on… Fate and Superstition; Family and Relationships; Violence.

Act Two:
NARRATOR: *"You don't even notice broken bottles in the sand, the oil in the water and you can't understand, how living could be anything other than a dream when you're young, free and innocent and just eighteen."*

Interpretation: In a scene where we see pure, untainted friendship and joy between the three youngsters, the narrator reminds the audience of the tainted world around them.

Techniques: Alliteration; Tri-colon; Imagery; Juxtaposition.

Analysis:
- The harsh, aggressive alliteration and imagery of "broken bottles" contrasts with the childish fun of "sand" – childhood becomes littered with danger.
- Unlike twins who are paired forever, "oil in the water" will never mix, with the pure "water" being stained by the dirty, destructive "oil".
- "A dream" highlights the unrealistic view of the world children have as they are "young" (suggesting inexperienced), "free" (suggesting unburdened by bills, jobs and responsibility), and "innocent" (implying naïve to the harshness of society).

Use in essays on…Truth; Education; Wealth; Family and Relationships.

Act Two:
> **NARRATOR:** "It was one day in October when the sun began to fade, and Winter broke the promise that Summer had just made, it was one day in October when the rain came falling down."

Interpretation: As time continues to move on, signified by the changing of the seasons, the promise and potential of youth fades for the working-class twin.

Techniques: Symbolism; Personification; Pathetic Fallacy; Repetition.

Analysis:
- The fact that the "sun", a symbol of life, optimism and growth, "began to fade", is representative of Mickey's life now taking a significant turn for the worse.
- The personified seasons imply that even nature works against Mickey. "Summer" may make a "promise" but is defeated by the onset of "Winter"; the repetition of "one day" stresses the speed with which life can change.
- The weather clearly mimics the action of the play – Mickey asking Linda out is "the sun", but from now on there will be nothing but "rain" in their life.

Use in essays on… Fate and Superstition; Truth.

Act Two:
EDWARD: "If I couldn't get a job I'd just say, sod it and draw the dole, live like a bohemian, tilt my hat to the world and say 'screw you'."

Interpretation: The class difference between Mickey and Edward is evident. Edward cannot empathise with Mickey's sense of personal failure, nor the extent of his poverty.

Techniques: Alliteration; Register; Imagery.

Analysis:
- The alliterative "draw the dole" suggests an easy lifestyle, but Edward does not grasp the social and personal consequences of being on the "dole".
- Edward's register is an unconvincing attempt at informality. "Sod it" and "screw you" show how unrealistic it is that Edward would ever have to face what Mickey faces, particularly when Mickey is "fucked off from everywhere".
- The imagery of "tilt my hat" and "live like a bohemian" have jovial, carefree associations, juxtaposed with the fact Mickey feels like he can do nothing but "crawl" and doesn't have the money to even "wear a hat", let alone "tilt" one.

Use in essays on… Education; Class; Wealth; Nature vs Nurture.

Act Two:
 MICKEY: "Not a job, not a house, nothin'. It used to be just sweets an' ciggies he gave me, because I had none of me own. Now it's a job and a house."

Interpretation: Traditional associations of twins, naturally connected, always acting as one, are shattered. Mickey is entirely dependent on Edward, even in adulthood.

Techniques: Tri-colon; Juxtaposition; Pronouns.

Analysis:
- Mickey's failure in life is emphasised by the tri-colon of elements he can't provide – he fails Linda economically ("a job"), as a husband who provides for his family ("a house") and as a useful member of society ("nothin'").
- The economic and class divide between Mickey and Edward was always clear, yet "sweets an' ciggies" have associations of a friend lending another friend something simple, juxtaposed to the grand, life-changing "job and a house".
- Mickey and Edward are twins, are blood brothers, but as we come to the end of the play, they are two separate individuals – "he" and "me".

Use in essays on… Family and Relationships; Nature vs Nurture; Wealth; Education.

Act Two:
 NARRATOR: "The girl would sing the melody but the woman stands in doubt and wonders what the price would be for letting the young girl out."

Interpretation: Linda is also a victim of choices made earlier in the play. Society dictates she must end up with Mickey, but her heart is torn between both brothers.

Techniques: Language; Juxtaposition.

Analysis:
- The active verb "sing" is dramatically different to Linda's current state, where she passively "stands in doubt".
- As a child Linda was carefree; her previous "melody" has associations with joy and vibrancy, juxtaposed with the depressing tone of "doubt" and "wonders".
- Linda does have a choice and could be independent by "letting the young girl out" and choosing Edward over Mickey. However, "letting" and "out" depict a state of imprisonment, and any refusal to conform to the life society has given her will come with a threatening "price".

Use in essays on… Class; Family and Relationships; Wealth.

Act Two:
NARRATOR: "You know he's right beside you, He's screamin' deep inside you."

Interpretation: The devil's stalking and hunting of its prey has come to an end – it is now time to pay the inevitable price of the deal that was made at the outset of the play.

Techniques: Verbs; Personification.

Analysis:
- "The devil" has stalked everyone throughout the play, but he is now ready to collect the debt. He is no longer "behind y'" but "beside you", and despite the fact "you know he's right beside you", there is nothing that can be done.
- The tense, intimidating verbs of "starin'" and "creepin'" from Act One have been replaced by the violent, aggressive "screamin'" – it is no longer a potential threat, but instead an inevitable outcome, and a violent one at that.
- Earlier, the devil was staring "through your windows" and was creeping "down the hall". Here, the devil has engulfed and consumed Mickey, taking over his entire being, as he is "deep inside" him.

Use in essays on… Fate and Superstition; Violence; Justice; Nature vs Nurture.

Act Two:
NARRATOR: *"And do we blame superstition for what came to pass? Or could it be what we, the English, have come to know as class?"*

Interpretation: Throughout the play the narrator has reinforced the idea that fate is the cause of the play's events; however, here the role of class and societal inequality is raised as the potential catalyst for the horror that has unfolded.

Techniques: Questioning; Repetition; Rhyme; Sentence Structure.

Analysis:
- Russell does not blame the Johnstones for the outcome of the play. The rhyme and sentence structure stress "class", implying society may be at fault.
- Furthermore, the repetition of "we" and the direct address to the audience seems to cast some responsibility upon those watching – since we maintain the class system, we must take the blame for the consequences that result.
- The message of the play is clear – since there is "blame", there must also be a guilty party, and for Russell it is "the English" and their class system.

Use in essays on… Class; Fate and Superstition; Truth.

Major Themes

Fate and Superstition
Truth
Violence

Nature versus Nurture
Class
Education

Family and Relationships
Wealth
Justice

Major Characters

Mrs Johnstone

Narrator

Sammy

Mickey

Edward

Linda

Mrs Lyons

Mr Lyons

Chorus

How to revise effectively.

One mistake people often make is to try to revise EVERYTHING!

This is clearly not possible.

Instead, once you know and understand the plot, a great idea is to pick three or four major themes, and three or four major characters, and revise these in great detail.

If, for example, you revised Mickey and Violence, you will also have covered a huge amount of material to use in questions about Class, Wealth or Family.

Or, if you revised Edward and Nature versus Nurture, you would certainly have plenty of material if a question on Mrs Johnstone, Fate or Education was set.

Use the following framework as a basis for setting *any* of your own revision questions – simply swap the theme or character to create a new essay title!

How does Russell portray the theme of _____ in *Blood Brothers*?

How does the character of _____ develop as the play progresses?

A sample essay paragraph (top level), using ideas directly from The Quotation Bank (page 16).

How does Russell present Class in Blood Brothers?

The difference between the classes is accentuated by the interactions with the policeman in Act One. After catching Mickey, Edward and Linda committing acts of vandalism, Mickey's mother is addressed as nothing more than "Missis", whereas Edward's father, because of his middle-class status, is addressed as "Mr Lyons". The policeman explains that "as I say, it was more of a prank, really, Mr Lyons. I'd just dock his pocket money if I was you"; the multi-clause sentence creates a sense of subservience towards Mr Lyons, and the submissive tone of "An' er, I say" stresses the fact the policeman is below him in the social hierarchy – the policeman's role is to protect the middle class and punish the working class. Furthermore, the intimidating threat of "courts, or worse" for Mrs Johnstone becomes a gentle docking of "pocket money" for Edward, highlighting the prejudice evident towards the working class in the legal system. Finally, Mickey's "serious crime" has become Edward's "prank". What was seen as violent, adult lawbreaking has morphed into a childish, somewhat amusing game, simply due to class discrimination.

Potential Essay Questions

How is family depicted in *Blood Brothers*?

Topic Sentence 1: The audience are shown that the natural bond between a mother and son can never be broken.

Use: Pages 17 and 18.

Topic Sentence 2: In contrast, the unnatural deal made by Mrs Lyons means that she never feels comfortable with the relationship between herself and Edward.

Use: Pages 10 and 19.

Topic Sentence 3: Furthermore, family should provide a sense of security, but often it creates isolation, secrecy and loneliness.

Use: Pages 21 and 23.

Topic Sentence 4: Family frequently leaves people with difficult decisions to face.

Use: Pages 9 and 29.

What is the significance of nature and nurture in the play?

Topic Sentence 1: Edward is nurtured in a formal, wealthy, middle class setting, presenting him with a strong education and a comfortable lifestyle.

Use: Pages 7 and 13.

Topic Sentence 2: In contrast, Mickey is surrounded by childish games, informal language and working-class troubles.

Use: Pages 9 and 14.

Topic Sentence 3: As a consequence, Edward is ready and able to face the world, whereas Mickey struggles to cope with life's pressures.

Use: Pages 22 and 27.

Topic Sentence 4: Despite the vastly different upbringings, Mickey and Edward are so similar in nature that Linda cannot choose between them.

Use: Pages 11 and 29.

How does the relationship between Mickey and Edward develop?

Topic Sentence 1: For the audience, the relationship between Mickey and Edward is one that has a constant sense of doom hanging over it.

Use: Pages 10 and 11.

Topic Sentence 2: Nonetheless, they are the best of friends, unburdened by class prejudice and free to act as they wish.

Use: Pages 24 and 25.

Topic Sentence 3: Yet, however close their bond is, society will always treat them differently because of their class status.

Use: Pages 15 and 16.

Topic Sentence 4: As time moves on, their upbringing tears them apart – their relationship cannot withstand the class differences that separate them.

Use: Pages 27 and 28.

What is the significance of fate in the play?

Topic Sentence 1: Whilst Mrs Johnstone's seemingly naïve belief in fate seems innocent enough, it leaves her open to manipulation by Mrs Lyons.

Use: Pages 8 and 10.

Topic Sentence 2: As the play proceeds, fate seems to grow in importance, always lurking in the background, stalking the characters.

Use: Pages 12 and 26.

Topic Sentence 3: Fate always wants to claim something – there is a price that needs to be paid, and it is inevitable that the outstanding debt will be collected.

Use: Pages 20 and 24.

Topic Sentence 4: Whilst fate is a violent, unstoppable force, Russell makes it clear to the audience that it is not entirely to blame for the outcome of the play.

Use: Pages 30 and 31.

Suggested Revision Activities

Major character and themes – Take any of the major characters and themes (see page 32 for a list) and group together quotations in sets of 2 or 3 to answer the following question: "How does the theme/character develop as the play goes on?"

You should try to get 4 sets of quotations, giving you 8-12 overall.

A great cover and repeat exercise – Cover the whole page, apart from the quotation at the top. Can you now fill in the four sections in your exercise book without looking – Interpretations, Techniques, Analysis, Use in essays on…?

This also works really well as a revision activity with a friend – cover the whole card, apart from the quotation at the top. If you read out the quotation, can they tell you the four sections without looking – Interpretations, Techniques, Analysis, Use in essays on…?

"The Development Game" – Pick any quotation at random from The Quotation Bank and use it to create an essay question, and then create a focused topic sentence to start the essay. Next, find another appropriate quotation to develop your idea even further.

"The Contrast Game" – Follow the same rules as The Development Game, but instead of finding a quotation to support your idea, find a quotation that can be used to start a counter-argument.

Your very own Quotation Bank! Using the same headings and format as The Quotation Bank, find 10 more quotations from throughout the text (select them from many different sections of the text to help develop whole text knowledge) and create your own revision cards.

Essay writing – They aren't always fun, but writing essays is great revision. Choose a practice question and then try taking three quotations and writing out a perfect paragraph, making sure you add connectives, technical vocabulary and sophisticated language.

Glossary

Alliteration – Repetition of the same consonant or sound at the beginning of a number of words in a sentence: the alliteration of "price she'll pay" is violent and aggressive, stressing the fact that fate will destroy everyone.

Dramatic Irony – When the audience knows something the characters don't: the dramatic irony of Edward's question "don't you have secrets" creates a great deal of tension in the audience.

Imagery – Figurative language that appeals to the senses of the audience: the imagery of "broken bottles" highlights how childhood becomes littered with danger.

Irony – A statement that suggests one thing but often has a contrary meaning: moving to the country to avoid "muck" and "dirt" is ironic. Mrs Johnstone does not mind the literal dirt - it is the metaphorical "muck" and "dirt" that plagues her.

Juxtaposition – Two ideas, images or words placed next to each other to create a contrasting effect: the formal "fornicate" juxtaposes the immature tone of "pimples" and "bum", which emphasises the conflict between childhood and adulthood.

Language – The vocabulary chosen to create effect.

Pathetic Fallacy – The weather or environment mimics the mood or actions of the play to enhance the effect: Mickey asking Linda out is "the sun", but from then on there is nothing but "rain" in their life.

Personification – A non-human object or concept takes on human qualities to make its presence more vivid to the audience: "Summer" may make a "promise" but is defeated by the onset of "Winter".

Polysyndeton – The repetition of conjunctions such as "and" one after another: Mickey's use of polysyndeton mimics the fact that, as he enters adolescence, his life becomes uncontrollable, seemingly slipping from his control.

Register – The type and style of language used in a particular social context (for example, formal or informal language): the vulgar "Pissed off" juxtaposes the refined "smashing", with the different registers stressing the class difference between Mickey and Edward.

Repetition – When a word, phrase or idea is repeated to reinforce it: Edward's repetition of "secrets" reinforces the underlying tension of the play.

Sentence Structure – The way the writer has ordered the words in a sentence to create a certain effect: the single clause sentence "But I won't" is strong and defiant in tone.

Sibilance – A variation on alliteration, usually of the 's' sound, that creates a hissing sound: the sibilance of "salt's been spilled" accentuates the speed with which things can go wrong – one small mistake and things spill out of control.

Symbolism – The use of a symbol to represent an idea: the reference to Mickey, Edward and Linda as "lambs" symbolises their innocence and purity, but also alludes to the metaphor of 'lambs to the slaughter'.

Tri-colon – A list of three words or phrases for effect: Mickey's failure in life is emphasised by the tri-colon of elements he can't provide – he fails Linda economically ("a job"), as a husband who provides for his family ("a house") and as a useful member of society ("nothin'").